SO-ANQ-355
9.95

Seasons of the Church Activities

Intermediate Level

created by Elizabeth Wells and Lisa Trout

God's Gifts Reproducible Activity Series
E.T. Nedder Publishing

Elizabeth Wells is a full-time, free-lance writer and editor who over the past 10 years has written several books and hundreds of articles for both the adult and childrens market. She received a Bachelor of Arts degree in Interdisciplinary Studies from the University of Nebraska at Omaha. The product of Catholic education, she and her husband are active in their three children's schools.

Lisa Trout has been a free-lance writer and illustrator for 10 years. Her work has been published in magazines and newspapers across the country. She earned a BA in the Distributed Studies of art, English, and psychology from Iowa State University. She teaches kindergarten Sunday School and is happily married with three wonderful children.

Cover Design: Fun `N Faith, LP
Editor: Kate Harrison

Copyright ©2001 E.T. Nedder Publishing
All rights reserved.

Except for the reproducible Masters, no part of this book may be reprinted or transmitted in any form or by any means, electronic or mechanical, or by an information retrieval system without permission in writing from the publisher. Reproducible pages are for classroom use only.

Additional copies of this publication may be produced by sending check or money order for $9.95 plus $4.00 postage and handling to: E.T. NEDDER Publishing, PMB 299, 9121 East Tanque Verde STE 105, Tuscon, Arizona 85749-8930. Or call toll free 1-877-817-2742. Fax: 1-520-760-5883. Email: RINGTAIL@prodigy.net

ISBN 1-893757-21-8

10 9 8 7 6 5 4 3 2

Dear Teacher,

Just like the seasons of the calendar year, the liturgical seasons are rich and diverse. Although the primary focus – that of growing closer to God – remains constant, each liturgical season offers change and renewal. Creating an early understanding of these seasons allows children to develop deep roots in Catholic tradition.

The following are some suggestions for making these pages a fun, faith-filled experience for you and your students.

Page 5

The simplified liturgical calendar can be used once or laminated for multiple uses. Continuous use lets the students experience the "big" picture. The circle represents something without a beginning or an ending. Its continuous nature provides a springboard to discussing God, who was in the beginning, is now and ever shall be, world without end.

It also serves as a great study tool. The students can color the wheel to represent the seasons and their corresponding colors. Review is simplified with its use.

Pages 6, 11, 16, 21, 24, 26, 29

Each of these pages serves as an introduction to the liturgical season it represents. In addition to the information on the page about the season, the students are encouraged to color the priest's vestments and the altar linens in the appropriate colors. Each page also has a puzzle or other activity that incorporates important information about the season.

While the students color the priest's vestments, you can talk about their names – the stole and the chasuble.

Page 7

This is a way for the students to reflect on how they are spending their Advent. Also connected is the topic of evangelizing to others through our works.

Page 8

Discuss the things we do for others. Remind the students that the coupons are just a starting point. Silent deeds are also appropriate during Advent and year-round.

Page 10

This activity is great either preceding or following a Jesse Tree activity. Also consider other family tree activities such as a written history or interviewing an older relative.

Page 11

Answer to puzzle: Star - Guided the Wise Men to Baby Jesus; Candy Cane - Shepherd's Staff, Blood of Christ; White - Purity, Joy and Triumph; Wreath - No Beginning, No End; Evergreens - Everlasting Life; Presents - God's Only Son; Candle - Light of the World.

This page is great for discussing the origins of some of the symbols. This shows a part of both the secular and religious holiday evolution.

Page 12

Help the students understand the angel's message and our ability to share that same message with others.

Page 13

Remind the students that gifts come in many shapes and sizes. They look different too. Talk about using our gifts and how we, as stewards of these gifts, need to return them to God.

You could hold a prayer service following this activity. The students could place their boxes on the altar symbolizing their acceptance of and need to give back to God.

Page 14

Help the students understand the similarities of the Apostles' Creed and our Baptismal vows.

Page 15

We develop tolerance of others in many ways. Help the students understand that knowledge helps us explain our differences and recognize our similarities.

Page 17

Explain that the sacrament of Reconciliation also removes the darkness of sin from our lives. It also allows our beauty as God's children to shine through.

Page 18

As a way to share the level of commitment to offer sacrifice during Lent, the students can present their palm on the altar either at church or in the classroom. Help them understand the significance of giving our sacrifice to God and how His grace helps us do even the most difficult things.

Page 19

God has given us many ways to resist the temptation of sin. Help the students gain a better understanding of these gifts, such as reading the Word, praying and receiving the sacraments. How can they use them to avoid sin?

Page 20

Easy access to the Bible really get the kids moving on this activity. You may have them make several and encourage them to display the stones. Ask them to share why they selected the scripture passages that they did.

Page 21

Answers:
Holy Thursday
Upper room
Breaking of the bread
Sharing the wine
Washing of the feet
Gethsemane
Jesus tells of his betrayal

Good Friday
Jesus taken away by guard
Tried before the Sanhedrin

For classroom use only © E. T. NEDDER Publishing

Jesus stands before Herod and Pilot
Jesus is scourged and condemned to die
Jesus carries the Cross
Jesus falls three times
Jesus is nailed to the Cross
Jesus dies and is laid in the tomb

Holy Saturday and Easter Vigil
Waiting
The women go to the tomb
Jesus is missing
The angel tells them He is risen
Peter and John go to the tomb
Jesus visits His disciples

Page 23

Help the students gain a better understanding of standing up for Christ. What ways do we deny the Christ in others by looking the other way? This includes standing up for others when they are being hurt.

Page 25

1. Jesus Is <u>Condemned</u> to <u>Death</u>
2. Jesus <u>Accepts</u> His <u>Cross</u>
3. Jesus <u>Falls</u>
4. Jesus <u>Meets</u> His <u>Mother</u>
5. <u>Simon</u> <u>Takes</u> the Cross
6. <u>Veronica</u> Wipes the <u>Face</u> of Jesus
7. Jesus <u>Falls</u> the Second Time
8. Jesus Meets the <u>Women</u>
9. Jesus Falls a <u>Third</u> Time
10. Jesus Is <u>Stripped</u> of His <u>Clothes</u>
11. Jesus Is <u>Nailed</u> to the Cross
12. Jesus <u>Dies</u>
13. Jesus Is <u>Removed</u> from the <u>Cross</u>
14. Jesus Is <u>Buried</u>
15. Jesus Is <u>Risen</u> from the <u>Dead</u>

Page 27

You will discover a star within the apple. Talk about the following apple legend. The apple reminds us that death can be followed by new life. The apple is similar to the fruit that Adam and Eve were told not to eat. When they disobeyed and ate the apple, they lost paradise.

God sent His Son, Jesus, to help us. He tells us that if we love Him and live our lives like His son, we will enter paradise after death.

As part of His promise, He left us a sign within the apple.

Page 28

This is a great jumping off point for a deeper discussion of the Holy Spirit and His gifts, the Trinity and evangelization.

Page 30

Help the students see that each shirt is beautiful and unique. Relate this back to God in each of our lives and how beautiful and unique each of us are. If desired the students can add words of praise using fabric paint.

Page 31

The students should spend some time learning about the saint they write on their wheat head. A class presentation or discussion can help familiarize the students with many saints quickly.

Page 32

Help the students gain a deeper understanding of where they see God in creation and Jesus in others. The possibilities are limitless.

Answers to word-find page 16

Answers to word-find page 22

For classroom use only © E. T. NEDDER Publishing

Prepare Ye the Way of the Lord

The liturgical seasons of the Church help us to prepare a way for the Lord in our lives. Each season helps us remember parts of Jesus' life, death and resurrection. It is a chance to look at our own life and see how Jesus fits in it.

In the liturgical seasons chart below, add the colors of the Mass for each season. Cut out the arrow and attach it with a brad to the middle of the circle.

You can use your new liturgical seasons chart as you study each season.

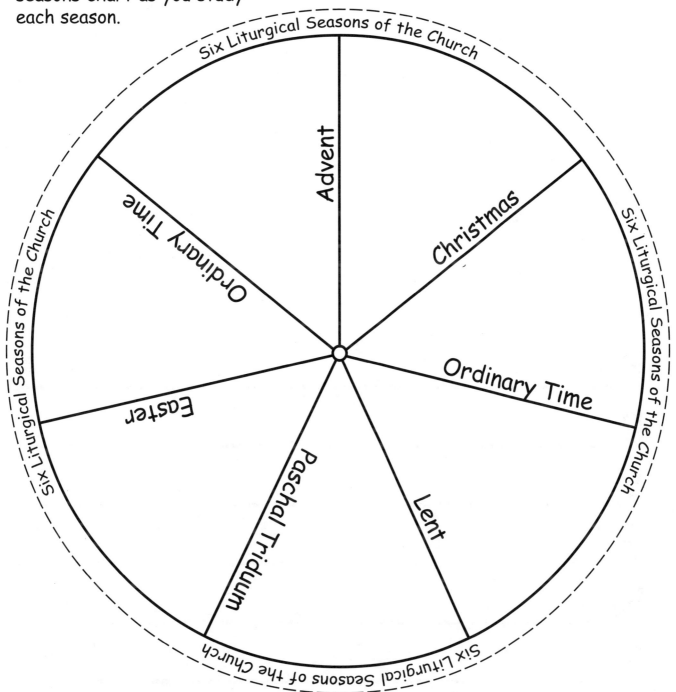

Advent

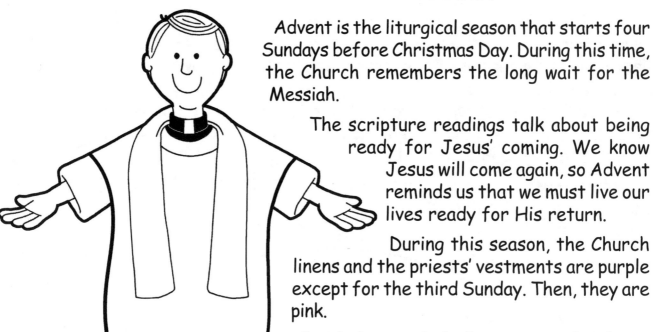

Advent is the liturgical season that starts four Sundays before Christmas Day. During this time, the Church remembers the long wait for the Messiah.

The scripture readings talk about being ready for Jesus' coming. We know Jesus will come again, so Advent reminds us that we must live our lives ready for His return.

During this season, the Church linens and the priests' vestments are purple except for the third Sunday. Then, they are pink.

Purple is a symbol of penance and pink is a symbol of joy. Advent is a time of joyful anticipation. At its end, we celebrate Christmas!

Create an Advent poem. Use the letters below to begin sentences that express the feelings, symbols and time of Advent.

A _____

D _____

V _____

E _____

N _____

T _____

Prepare Ye the Way of the Lord

During Advent, we focus on living our lives so that we are ready for Christ.

One way is to share Jesus' love with others. How are we Jesus to others?

We can prepare
for Jesus' birth by showing
His love through our actions. During
this time of preparing, write the good
works you do for others in the boxes.
Before you know it, you will be
celebrating Jesus' birth!

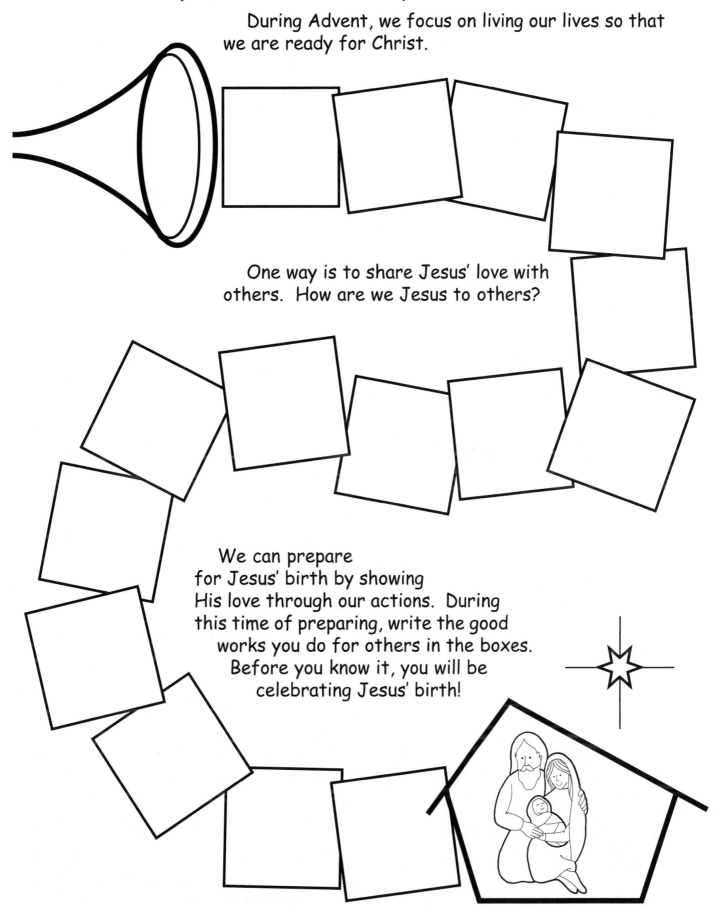

For classroom use only © E. T. NEDDER Publishing

Advent Coupons

One way to wait during Advent is to give gifts of self to others. When we give to others, we feel joy. There are several coupons for gifts of service or acts of kindness to others. Write the service or deed you will give on the first line. Sign your name on the second. When we share these kinds of gifts, others can see Christ through us and the miracle of Christmas lives!

Waiting in Faith

Waiting for something, especially something wonderful, can be hard. We want the time to go faster. We check to see how much time is left. We are anxious for the time to pass. Eventually the time arrives, and we are happy.

Soon we will celebrate the anniversary of Christ's birthday. His birth holds our promise of eternal life. During Advent, we are encouraged to grow in faith while we wait.

Each day, color one symbol with its color from the key. In a few days, you will discover several things that can help you grow in faith while you wait.

Day one – R (red)   Day four - G (green)
Day two – O (orange)   Day five - B (blue)
Day three - Y (yellow)   Day six - V (violet)

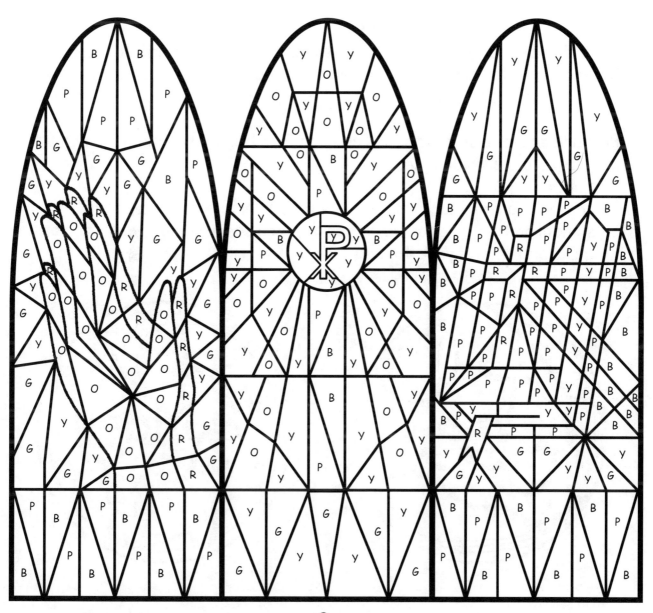

Family Trees

During Advent, many people make a Jesse Tree. The tree is made up of symbols of Jesus' family tree. It traces the ancestry and prophecy of the Messiah through the Bible. A traditional Jesse Tree looks like the picture to the right.

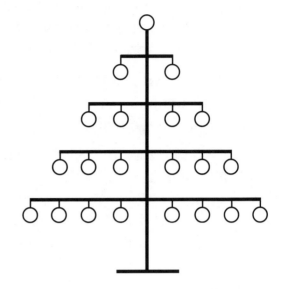

We remember the extreme gift of Jesus as our brother during Advent. This is also a good time to remember the gifts of our immediate family. Take a few moments to think about the people in your family. Which symbols would you use to express their gifts?

Prepare to make an ornament for each member by hot gluing a magnet on the back of a clean juice lid.

Using permanent markers, yarn, paper, fabric, glue and glitter, create that symbol on the juice can lid. When dry, you can assemble your tree on the refrigerator for everyone to see!

Christmas

The Christmas season begins with Christmas Day and continues until Epiphany. Epiphany is 12 days after Christmas.

At Christmas, we remember God's love and the gift He gave to us - His Son, Jesus Christ. Jesus became human to save us from the power of sin and death. We know that Jesus' gift of eternal life comes at a cost. He gave His life on the Cross.

During the Christmas season, priests wear white and gold vestments. The colors found in the sanctuary are also gold and white. White is the color we use to symbolize joy. Gold underscores the celebration.

Many of the decorations we use are symbols of faith. Unscramble the words in each column below, then draw lines to the things they symbolize.

— — — —
RTSA

Light of the World

— — — — — — — — —
DNCYA NEAC

Everlasting Life

— — — — —
ETHWI

No Beginning, No End

— — — — — —
AHRWET

Purity, Joy and Triumph

— — — — — — — — —
ENSGEVRERE

God's Only Son

— — — — — — — —
TSEPENRS

Shepherd's Staff, Blood of Christ

— — — — — —
LCDENA

Guided the Wise Men to Baby Jesus

For classroom use only © E. T. NEDDER Publishing

Let His Light Shine Through

On that first Christmas, the angels told the shepherds the news of Christ's birth. The news was so joyful that the shepherds had to learn more about the child who was their Savior.

We can share that Good News too! Christ came for everyone. Through our words and deeds, we can tell others that Christ was born and died so we can live. We do this whenever we let Christ's love of others shine through us.

Make the candle screen below to help you remember to let Christ's love shine through you - in your words and actions.

Cut a piece of foil 8 1/2" x 11" and then fold it in half to make it 8 1/2" x 5 1/2". Use the pattern below. Poke holes through the pattern and foil with a sharpened pencil. Fold the foil to create the screen.

With an adult's help, place a candle behind the screen and light it in a darkened room. The light symbolizes the Light of Christ and the angel reminds us to share Christ with others.

Gifts Come In Many Different Packages

Jesus' greatest gift is His death and resurrection. We receive eternal life because of His gift. We were given gifts by our heavenly Father. We need to share these with the world. (Lk 8:16)

What are your gifts? Below, write how you will share them with the world. Cut it out and place it in a box. Decorate the box using any of the following: paper, markers, crayons, glue, glitter, etc.

For classroom use only © E. T. NEDDER Publishing　　13

Baptism

During Christmas we remember that we too have a new birth in Christ through the sacrament of Baptism. The waters of baptism unite us with Christ in both life and death. Its grace helps us live in holiness.

The waters of baptism also set us free from the death of sin. During the sacrament of Baptism, the priest talks about the waters of the great flood and the waters of the Jordan River in which John baptized Jesus. He also talks about the water that flowed from Jesus' side when he was on the Cross.

These symbolic references to water link its cleansing power to the removal of sin. During baptism, the person being baptized or their god-parents are asked to live like Christ and to choose Christ over evil.

How do you refuse evil in your life?

_____
_____
_____

Do you believe in God the Father, Jesus Christ His Son, and the Holy Spirit?_____

How do you show that you believe?

_____
_____
_____

Do you believe in the Catholic Church, the communion of saints, the forgiveness of sins, the resurrection of the body and life everlasting?____

NEW LIFE

He Came for Everyone

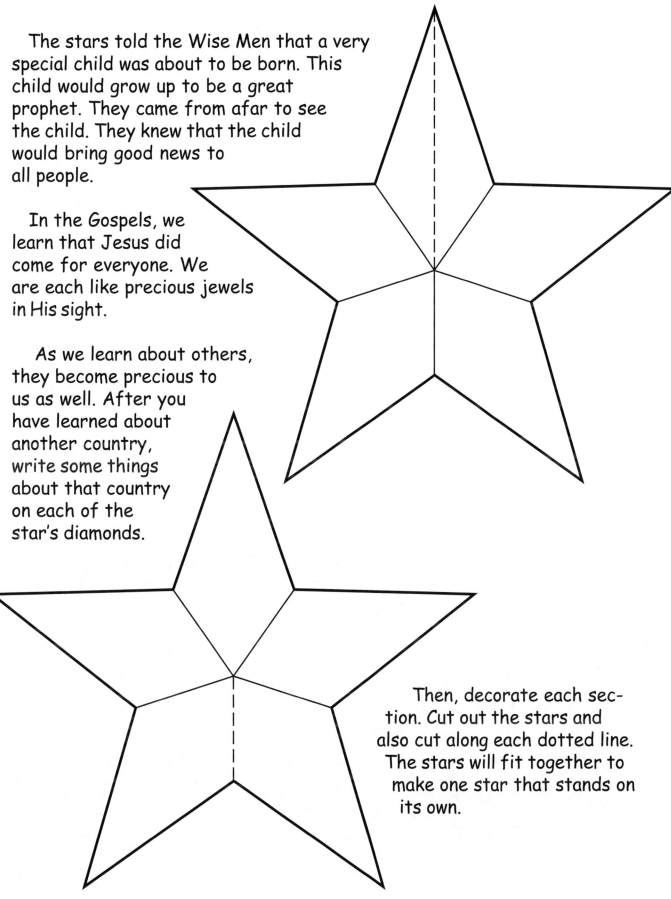

The stars told the Wise Men that a very special child was about to be born. This child would grow up to be a great prophet. They came from afar to see the child. They knew that the child would bring good news to all people.

In the Gospels, we learn that Jesus did come for everyone. We are each like precious jewels in His sight.

As we learn about others, they become precious to us as well. After you have learned about another country, write some things about that country on each of the star's diamonds.

Then, decorate each section. Cut out the stars and also cut along each dotted line. The stars will fit together to make one star that stands on its own.

For classroom use only © E. T. NEDDER Publishing   15

Lent

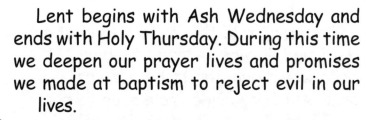

Lent begins with Ash Wednesday and ends with Holy Thursday. During this time we deepen our prayer lives and promises we made at baptism to reject evil in our lives.

We can deepen our prayer lives through reading the Bible and reflecting on the Word. Some people choose to fast, or give something up.

All of this prepares us for celebrating Christ's death and resurrection.

The colors of the linens and vestments are purple as a sign of penance. On the fourth Sunday of Lent, Laetare Sunday, the color is pink. We rejoice knowing that the celebration of God's mercy through Christ's death is only a few weeks away.

```
Y O P E C I F I R C A S
A N C G U J M K O T S R
K L E C T I O N S E A E
P F M P E U C R N R C F
R G Y S C Q P E T E R L
A N X O G R V U I Y T E
Y I E I H I O S N A M C
B T C A G N V T G R O T
L S Y R S A F I O R N I
M A O B H T R V N I T O
N F P E N A N C E G P N
```

Look for the following Lenten words in the word-find.

Almsgiving
Fasting
Forgiveness
Penance
Prayer
Reflection
Sacrifice

Prepare the Way—Lent

Lent is a time for us to look at the things in our life that keep us away from God's full love. Sometimes we focus all of our attention on things instead of our loving Father.

We use Lent to sharpen our focus on God by fasting and sacrifice. When God is our focus, we make better choices and sin less. Sin is like a black coating that keeps the colors of God's love from shining through us. Sharpen your focus by scratching through to the many wonderful colors of Christ.

Paint the box below with several bright watercolors. Next, take a black crayon and color over until all of the other colors are hidden. Then, using a wooden craft stick, scratch a drawing through the black crayon. Your colors will shine through!

Ash Wednesday

On Ash Wednesday, we remember that because we are human, all of us will die sometime. We remember that Christ died for us so that we might live forever.

Ash Wednesday begins the season of Lent. During this time, we are called to remove the things that get between God's love and us. We are also asked to make sacrifices as a way of remembering how much we really do have.

Think about the things that sometimes stand between you and receiving God's love. Using the "palm," write one of the things you will work on or "sacrifice" this Lent.

The ashes used on Ash Wednesday come from burning the palms we received on the last Palm Sunday.

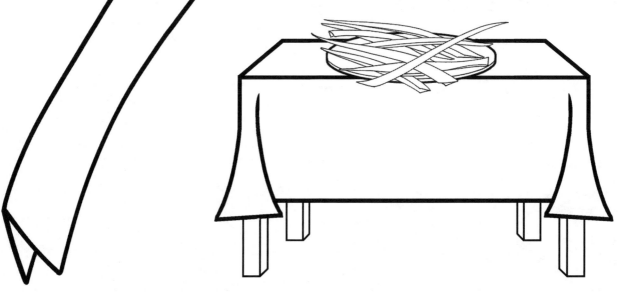

40 Days and 40 Nights

Even Jesus was tempted. He spent 40 days and 40 nights in the desert preparing. He removed the things that stood between Him and His Father by fasting.

At the end of this time, Satan tempted Jesus three times.

Read Matthew 4:1-11.

Sunday	Monday	Tuesday	Wednesday	Thursday	Friday	Saturday
			1	2	3 ◎	4
5	6	7	8	9	10	11
12		14	15	16	17	18
19		21	22	23	24	25
26		28	29	30	31	32
33		35	36	37	38	39
40						

What things tempt you to pull away from God's love? Write three temptations below.

What things can we do to avoid giving in to these temptations? Write them down too.

Stones to Bread

The Gospel tells us that Jesus fasted for 40 days and nights. He was very hungry when Satan said He could just say the word to turn the stones into bread (Matthew 4:1-4). Jesus knew that He needed more than just food for His body. He needed food for His soul too.

The Word of God provides us with food for our souls. The Bible gives us this food through the stories, proverbs and psalms.

Turn stones into bread – the kind for your soul!

Paint a rock with acrylic paint. Choose your favorite Bible verse or one listed below and write it on the rock using a permanent marker.

BLESSED ARE THE PEACEMAKERS MT 5:9

SEEK FIRST THE KINGDOM OF GOD.... MT 6:33

LOVE EACH OTHER MK 12:31

LORD HOW GLORIOUS IS YOUR NAME PS 8:2

Paschal Triduum

During the Paschal Triduum, we remember the Passion, Death and Resurrection of Jesus. Look at the list of events below and place them in order beneath the day on which we remember them.

Jesus carries the Cross
Waiting
Peter and John go to the tomb
Upper room
Jesus is nailed to the Cross
Jesus visits His disciples
Sharing the wine
Jesus dies and is laid in the tomb
Jesus is scourged and condemned to die
Gethsemane
Washing of the feet
The angel tells them He is risen
Jesus tells of his betrayal
The women go to the tomb
Jesus stands before Herod and Pilot
Breaking of the bread
Jesus falls three times
Tried before the Sanhedrin
Jesus is missing
Jesus taken away by guard

HOLY THURSDAY

_____

_____

_____

_____

_____

GOOD FRIDAY

_____

_____

_____

_____

_____

HOLY SATURDAY
AND EASTER VIGIL

_____

_____

_____

_____

_____

Holy Thursday
Breaking Bread Together

Because Jesus was Jewish, much of our faith has roots in the Jewish religion, Judaism. One of the important feast days in the Jewish religion is Passover.

Jesus and his disciples remembered Passover with a traditional dinner on what we call Holy Thursday. We call this The Last Supper. It was during the Last Supper that Jesus gave us the Eucharist.

Find the Passover words in the puzzle.

unleaven
bread
lamb
wine
covenant
prayer
tradition
Moses
Egypt
freedom
promise

```
N E N C O V E N E N T
M O U S N P A B L M R
O T U J H R M L P B A
S F I N S A D I T I D
E R T O L Y P S T M I
S A X B R E A D P G T
C R E E W R A V Y O I
F R E E D O M V G E O
D A E R V I E N E U N
P R O M I S E W I N E
```

I tell you I do not know this man!

During the Passion of our Lord, we remember that Peter was asked about his friendship with Jesus three times. Each time his fear prevented him from saying yes. He denied Jesus all three times.

Fear is a powerful emotion. We do not want people to hurt us, say bad things about us, or make fun of our actions. Sometimes these stand in the way of showing Christ to others.

What are some of the ways you deny Christ?_____

_____

How do you feel when this happens?_____

_____

After the third time Peter denied knowing Christ, the rooster crowed. The rooster wakes us up when we have fallen asleep. Peter remembered Christ's words when he heard the bird. He ran from the courtyard full of sadness.

When we "awake" to our own denial, we have the chance to make things better. How could you make things better if you find that you have denied Christ? _____

_____

Color and cut out the rooster. Tape it to your desk or bedroom door. This way it will be nearby offering its wake-up call.

Good Friday

"I will tear down the temple and build it up in three days," Jesus told the crowd at the temple. They were shocked because it had taken 40 years to build it. They did not understand that He was referring to the temple of his own body and its new life in the resurrection.

On Good Friday, we remember the many sacrifices Jesus endured for us. His peers unfairly judged him. When have we judged others unfairly?

People accused him unfairly. When have we unfairly blamed others?

His clothes were taken away. When have we taken other people's things unfairly?

He was beaten and made to carry the heavy burden of the Cross. When have we used our force or words to hurt others?

Others mocked him. When have we made fun of others? He was left to die. When have we walked away from another who is in need?

The Good News is that Jesus' death and resurrection frees us from the death of sin. On Good Friday, consider what sacrifices you can make as you remember the great gift He gives us. In the journal space below, write down some of the things you can do.

_____

_____

_____

_____

_____

_____

Stations of the Cross

On Good Friday, we remember Jesus' suffering, death, and resurrection through the Stations of the Cross. The Stations of the Cross are listed to the right. Use the maze below to help you find the missing words. Each line of the maze contains the next word for the list. Circle the word and write it on the blank line.

1. Jesus Is _____ to _____
2. Jesus _____ His _____
3. Jesus _____
4. Jesus _____ His _____
5. _____ _____ the Cross
6. _____ Wipes the _____ of Jesus
7. Jesus _____ the Second Time
8. Jesus Meets the _____
9. Jesus Falls a _____ Time
10. Jesus Is _____ of His _____
11. Jesus Is _____ to the Cross
12. Jesus _____
13. Jesus Is _____ from the _____
14. Jesus Is _____
15. Jesus Is _____ from the _____

START ➡		Condemned		Galilee
	Going		Death	Pontius Pilate
	Accepts		Declares	Wants
	Crime		Situation	Cross
	Wonders		Falls	Forgives
	Believes	Follows	Meets	Salutes
	Friends	Father	Brother	Mother
	Andrew	Judas	Simon	Joseph
	Takes	Uses	Borrows	Discovers
Martha	James	John	Veronica	Mary
Cross	Feet	Blood	Dirt	Face
Falls	Sneezes	Balances	Trips	
Apostles	People	Women	Prophets	
Another	Fifth	Second	Third	
Punished	Taunted	Stripped	Detached	
Things	Possessions	Strength	Clothes	
Nailed	Tied	Strapped		
Cries	Prays	Dies		
Removed	Borrowed	Detached		
Cave	Cross	Grave		
Buried	Hungry	Sad		
Taken	Risen	Removed		
Living	Dead	FINISH ➡		

Easter

Alleluia! Let all of heaven proclaim the Good News! He is risen!

Easter is the most joyful season in the liturgical year. Jesus' resurrection means that we too can live. Death no longer holds us. We can live forever with our Heavenly Father.

This joyful time is one in which we celebrate Christ's victory over death and evil.

We celebrate the Easter season for seven weeks. During this time, the priest's vestments and church linens are vibrant white and gold. These are colors of victory and great joy.

Write a word that uses each of the letters below to transform the cross. These words can explain or detail Christ's victory and our joy.

```
        R
        E
        S
        U
C H R I S T
        R
        E
        C
        T
        I
        O
        N
```

Death of a Seed

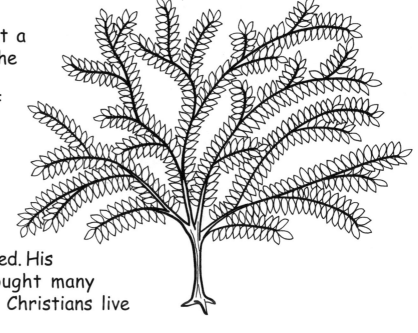

Jesus told a parable about a mustard seed. He said that the kingdom of God is like a mustard seed. This smallest of seeds can grow into a huge shrub. It is so large that even birds build their nests in its branches.
(Mt 13:31-32)

Jesus is like the mustard seed. His death and resurrection brought many people to His Father. Today Christians live across the entire world.

One seed can really produce great fruit. Cut an apple in half through the middle.

What do you see?

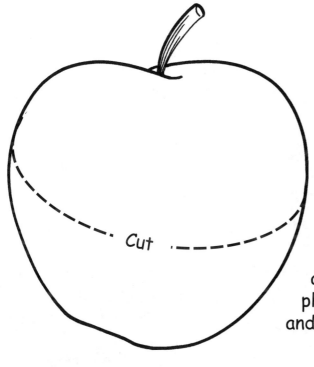

Cut

Take a few seeds and plant them in a clean milk carton filled with soil.

Make sure your seed receives the right mix of water and sunlight.

When your seed grows into a seedling, ask your parents or principal if there is a place to plant your apple tree. This way you and others can enjoy its fruit in future years.

Pentecost - Gifts of the Spirit

When Jesus returned to His Father in heaven, His disciples were afraid. They hid in the Upper Room.

Jesus promised them that He would send them help. He sent the Holy Spirit. The Holy Spirit brings us gifts to love the Father. The colors of the rainbow help us remember these gifts.

Wisdom
Understanding
Knowledge
Counsel
Piety
Fortitude
Fear

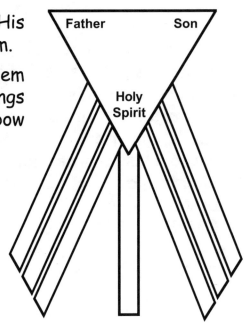

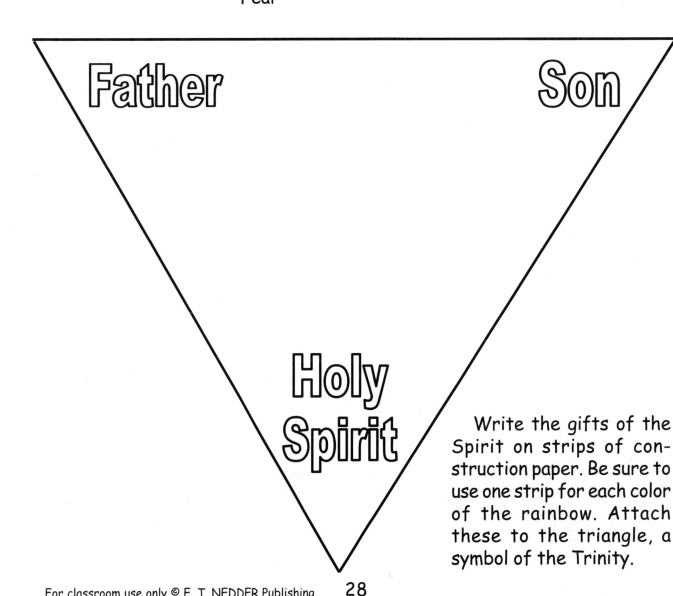

Write the gifts of the Spirit on strips of construction paper. Be sure to use one strip for each color of the rainbow. Attach these to the triangle, a symbol of the Trinity.

Ordinary Time

Recognizing God in "ordinary" time feeds our souls. When we recognize that He is in everything around us, how can we be anything but joy-filled.

Joy is a sign of God. Ordinary time allows us to see God's finger-prints in our daily life.

It is a time when we can grow closer to Him because our joy simply cries out, and we must praise the one who gives us every gift and blessing!

What are some of the ordinary times in your life? Can you think of any that have made good memories? Write them down below. Take time to remember the details. Include them too.

_____

_____

_____

_____

_____

_____

_____

_____

_____

_____

Nothing Ordinary about Ordinary Time

Spread the Word. God loves us and gives us every grace and blessing! Pretty amazing, but who have you told lately? Ordinary time gives us a chance to see God in our daily lives and to share His presence with others.

God is busy creating masterpieces of our lives. He takes us wherever we are. We do not know what the end result will be. But if we accept Him in our lives, He will work wonders.

Follow the directions below to create a masterpiece of your own. Like the t-shirt absorbing color, if we accept God in our lives, the results are amazing.

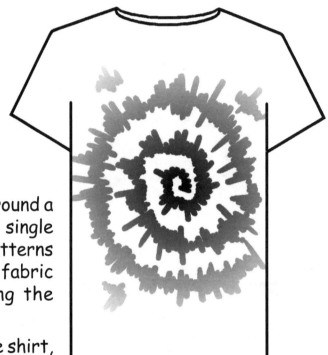

Supplies
Prewashed t-shirt
Clothing dyes
Rubberbands
Plastic squeeze bottles
Water
Vinegar

1. Begin by twisting rubberbands around a prewashed t-shirt. Tie off only a single layer to achieve the best results. Patterns may be achieved by leaving t-shirt fabric between rubberbands and putting the rubberbands in different places

2. Once finished rubberbanding the shirt, pour dye into plastic squeeze bottles.

3. Squeeze dye onto fabric between rubberbands. Alternating colors will achieve interesting results.

4. Allow shirt to dry completely.

5. Remove rubberbands.

NOTE: Before wearing or washing, soak shirts in a 2-to-1 water and vinegar bath to set the colors. Be safe. DO NOT WASH SHIRT WITH OTHER CLOTHING FOR AT LEAST THE FIRST WASHING TO PREVENT COLOR TRANSFER.

Now use your shirt to help spread the Good News. Whenever anyone comments on your shirt tell them about God working in your life. His love in your life is a masterpiece.

For classroom use only © E. T. NEDDER Publishing

Harvest of Holiness

During Ordinary Time, we celebrate many Feast Days and Holy Days. The Saints' Feast Days are important examples of holy lives. Holy Days provide celebrations of our faith.

Using a Church calendar, write down a couple of these special celebrations on the backs of the wheat heads below. Cut them out and attach to a pipe cleaner as shown.

Wheat provides us with many different kinds of foods. In our faith, wheat is a symbol of life-giving bread because it makes the Eucharist. The Saints' lives provide food for thought. The Holy Days provide life-giving Good News!

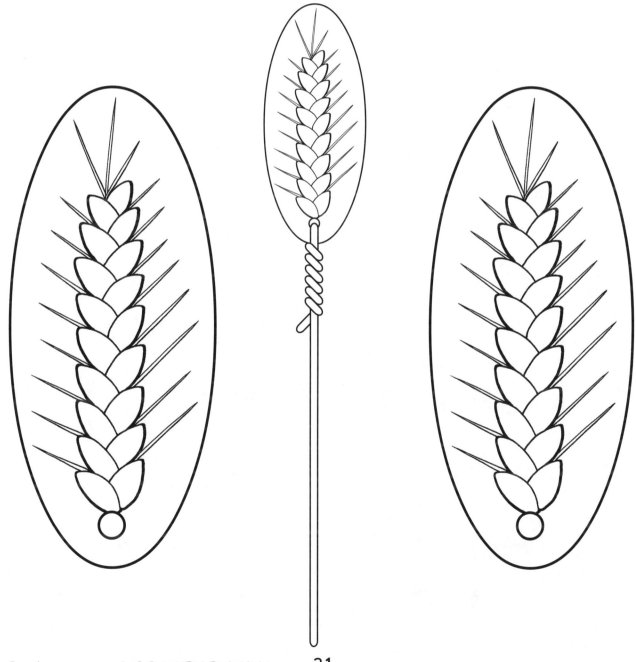

Food for Life

We think of God as creator and Jesus as brother. Where do you see God's fingerprints in your daily life?_____

_____

_____

Where do you meet Jesus?_____

_____

_____

Find examples of these in magazines, photographs or your own drawings and glue them to an 8 1/2" x 11" piece of paper. Cut a frame for your "Picture of Praise" from a larger piece of cardstock. Decorate your frame by gluing a variety of seeds and grains to the cardstock. Remember how God nourishes us.

For classroom use only © E. T. NEDDER Publishing